COLD HEARTED WITH A TENDER SOUL LIFE IN MY DARKEST MOMENTS BEHIND BARS

JAAMI R. LAMAR

outskirts press

Cold Hearted with a Tender Soul
Life In My Darkest Moments Behind Bars
All Rights Reserved.
Copyright © 2021 Jaami R. Lamar
v1.0

This is a work of fiction. The events and characters described herein are imaginary and are not intended to refer to specific places or living persons. The opinions expressed in this manuscript are solely the opinions of the author and do not represent the opinions or thoughts of the publisher. The author has represented and warranted full ownership and/or legal right to publish all the materials in this book.

This book may not be reproduced, transmitted, or stored in whole or in part by any means, including graphic, electronic, or mechanical without the express written consent of the publisher except in the case of brief quotations embodied in critical articles and reviews.

Outskirts Press, Inc.
http://www.outskirtspress.com

Paperback ISBN: 978-1-9772-4167-2

Cover Photo © 2021 www.gettyimages.com. All rights reserved - used with permission.

Outskirts Press and the "OP" logo are trademarks belonging to Outskirts Press, Inc.

PRINTED IN THE UNITED STATES OF AMERICA

Table of Contents

What Instrument Are U?	1
2 Parents-n-1	2
"Lonely Moments"	3
Listen	4
"Product of my Environment"	6
Mistaken Identity	8
Random Thoughts	9
False Tales	10
Fire & Desire	11
Lights, Camera, Action	12
Rocky	13
Old Faithful	14
Is there a difference between "Love & Luv"	15
"I Did It for the Love"	17
I Do	18
"Growth & Maturity"	19
Should I Ever	21
Shell Shocked	23
"State of Incarceration"	24
Magnetic Connection	25
Happily Dedicated	26
Safe	27
Uncovering Verse Discovery	28
My Brother is your Brother	29
" The law of Attraction"	30
Love Doctor X	32
Say Her Name, Say Her Name	33

"Uncertainties"	34
Can't help but wait...	36
The Inability And Incapability To Love Never Allow Your Past To Define You...	37
"The Everlasting Impression of on Incarcerated Mind of Man"	40
Acknowledgements/ Thank You's	42

What Instrument Are U?

The definition of an instrument is as follows:

*A means by which something is accomplished.

*A device for recording, indicating or measuring in a controlled system.

    The instrument I proclaim to be is the heart. I chose this instrument because it's essential to living life. Some may argue that the brain controls the body and that is absolutely correct. However, if you go brain dead the heart still pumps. But if your heart dies, you die period. The heart feels and desires emotional care once attached. Deeply intertwined hearts are dangerously amazing. So to me I feel this instrument is most important above all else.

My heart pounds for you
Yours pound for me
They both are pounding for love from each other ultimately.

2 Parents-n-1

To all mothers who have deadbeat baby daddies...
Keep doing your best to provide for your children. It's a true blessing to see all your hard work pay off. It's the fathers lost.

She painfully pushed me out of her womb
She showed me how to properly clean my room
He taught me my first words
He showed me how to pop a wheelie on the curb
She gave me hugs and kisses to express her unconditional love
She punished me when I was wrong
'Cause that too expressed love
He dressed me to impress
He taught me to always do my best
She never turned her back or gave up on me
She always believed in me
He showed me how to treat a female
He respected her and they both taught me well
She actually was He, while He lost out knowing me.

"Lonely Moments"

Days I wake up wishing I was lying next to you
Always finding myself asking simple questions
Your love must stay true, it gets better in due time
Sooner than later we will reunite

Another day passes me by and my nights are filled with lonely moments
Why should I stress over situations I can't handle?
And who really cares about my lonely stressful days?
You!

For all it's worth, I really do believe it will work
Real love is hard to find and it's truly blind
Only time will tell if it's meant to be
Most lonely moments are spent reading your letters

Your words are so sincere that they make my soul quiver
One day this nightmare will all be over
Until then I must face more lonely moments to come

Listen

Can you hear me???
I guess I'm just another statistic for the hood.
Young and thuggin,' doing time for head busting.
Hoodlums as they say, are always the topics of discussion.
I guess society is Donald Trump and the less fortunate are the Russians.
Hate it or love it, but I will survive.
Constantly building on the up rise.
Raised in the streets,
Became familiar with the speech...
Of stocks, bonds, and, politics, but don't be surprised
That I strive for greatness with pain in my eyes.
From all of the deception, betrayal, and lies,
I bet you judged this book by it's cover.
Knowledge and wisdom are powers you'll soon discover.
What's done in the dark must be shown in the light.
An epidemic of heroin is killing the whites,
When crack and needles have taken the likes
Of black mothers and fathers who paid with their life
Oh so now there's a problem? Yeah right!
Who came to the rescue when we had to fight?
Let me guess... not a damn soul!
These stereotypes are getting so tired and old.
I know Christians and Muslims with life on parole.
A couple a bloods and crips who are stuck in the hole,
That takes no disrespect while reppin their set.
Respect it or not the police are receiving a check,
For killing, protecting, and reppin their set.
The biggest organized criminal enterprise there is,

For centuries and decades, over years and years.
Now stopping in traffic are filled with the fear,
Of innocents, goosebumps, chills, and tears.
Because one sudden move is declared a justified kill,
Open your eyes wide. Clear your ears.
Can you hear me now??? Good...

"Product of my Environment"

I'm from the hood, where u either played sports or sold dope.
Product of my environment... Just another lost boy with no hope.
Infatuated with the showboat,
Hundred dollar bills and gold ropes.
"That boy's going to end up dead" says the old folks.
Reality sets in fast. This shit is no joke!
Never would've envisioned being imprisoned.
Where strip searches and public shitting is daily living.
Privacy and luxuries are forbidden.
Gourmet meals out the kitchen bullshitting, I'm just kidding,
Gossiping, bickering men sounding like women.
Portraying an image they wanted, but never was living,
I'm from the hood where u become the victim, or victimizer.
Learning to become the struggle through early survival,
Middle school drop out to pharmaceutical provider,
No ambition or motivation that will get you hired.
Either you kill, hesitate and add to the death toll.
Lost lives deprived of proper guidance adds to another fallen soul.
Now it's "Rest In Peace" faces printed out on T-shirts.
Old folks say, "value life for what it's worth, there's no comparison to the streets."
Never listening as we're cocaine flipping.
Quick way to the graveyard or prison.
Fatherless children,

Babymammas trippin,
Constantly down puttn', embedding lies knowing she shouldn't.
Want her child to follow the stereotypical footings
Of hoodlums, gangsters, and thugs...
Ever streets politicians,
Product of my environment to some extent just don't be afraid to
Be different.
To all the planted seeds of the world and our future children.

Mistaken Identity

Clearly the misrepresentation of me is a total facade.
Some might say I come off as a complete asshole.
At times a passive aggressive prick
An overly aggressive jerk.
I just respond by asking that individual to sit down and converse with me.
I'm a selfless & humble, kind-hearted & lovable, genuine man.
If I'm about you, I'm for you all the way.
No strings attached.
But if lines were ever crossed,
I will leave yo ass high and dry.
Opposites attract.
Differences in lifestyles, upbringings, cultural backgrounds, ect.
No smoking mirrors, no hidden agendas, I am who I am.
Up front. Straight forward. A true, one hundred percent honest guy.
Respect goes a long way.
Just because I don't disrespect you doesn't mean that I respect you.
Respect is earned not given.

My pain is real, my life is real.
Remember me... a product of my environment.
Facts only.
It all made me who I am.
Now that I've grown actually viewing things as they are and what they are worth, my vision is clear.

Random Thoughts

There are many dimensions of prison in which we as prisoners must succumb to degrading and devastating conditions or diminish them all together. We must adapt ourselves to uncomfortable environments sticking to previous reputations to maintain and or create an alternative persona and or attitude.

To some individuals, prison is time wasted, therefore time doing nothing. Just because my body is encaged doesn't mean my mind has to be as well. Keeping mental sanity is most important while imprisoned. It's often said that you can make the best out of a bad situation. That statement, to me, defines a person's will power as well as their motivation to surpass or see past the countless trials and tribulations we are faced with each day within this crooked system.

Growth and development are two critical factors if you are going to stay alive in this hectic world. We must put forth the effort to make sure there's a future for ourselves when released. Nobody's going to put forth the effort for you. Learning must be implemented into your daily routine. Remember, you're never too old to learn. Most individuals get stuck in a place of stagnation, never allowing themselves to potentially reach maturity.

False Tales

Before this I truly believed things would work between us
Reality soon set in as the lies got worst
Only you could make me feel weak and helpless when it comes to love
Keep on trying is what I keep telling myself
Even after the disrespect and betrayal
Never again will I play the fool

Problems will be handled but hearts aren't meant to be broken
Relationships are hard to manage if you can't trust the one you love
Often men can't admit to the pain that they suffered
Memories of betrayal is what I call it
I truly wonder if there's a soulmate for me
Stuck in this slump, I'll soon find my way out
Everybody deserves a good companion to settle down with
Some people will never find that perfect person

Fire & Desire

Spiritual connection is where our souls meet
Inhale, exhale... pleasantly scented
Mentally lifted... physically finished
Accepting her offers without a speech,
She consoles me oh so deep
Simply tasteful
Forever faithful
Never ungrateful
I can't keep my hands to myself in your presence
Things tend to heat up with every session
Stuck in a "Blue Dream" of "Purple Haze"
"4-20" is the day we engage
"This girl is on fire" & I'm so amazed
At how she climaxes in such a blaze
Reaching her peak quickly and fast
Til death do us apart I'm in love with that "Gas"
Puff, puff, pass. Puff, puff, pass.

Lights, Camera, Action

My life at times feels like a video game or some type of movie
Others may have found their purpose and are striving to succeed
Troublesome situations find themselves heading my way even though I stand clear of the bullshit
Invalid thoughts steadily cross my mind intoxicating my brain cells
Occupied with time, I always do my best to stay obedient to my laws as a man
Nervous about the next move I make because it would cost me my life

Previous experiences help me stand on my own
Always playing by principals
Intelligent and forever clever help me mentally to stand higher than normal
Cocky, Confident, Confused all describes me to a "T"
Temperamental with an uptight, troubled attitude
Unsure who to trust, leaves me frustrated
Regrets, I have none.
Learning from mistakes are lessons learned
Experiences of past struggles helps me excel beyond stereotypes

Rocky

Their are so many women in this world that are beautiful
Wonderful personalities are unique
Great smile, nice breast, pretty face...
Thick thighs, bubble butts, slim waist...
All these characteristics are within you.
I found my perfect lady, it's true.
If not you, then who?
She's smart & Sophisticated
Sassy & Silly
And of course she's Sexy.
Someone I finally consider my besty,
My lover, companion, and all in all good friend.
She's my rock. I'm her heartbeat.

Old Faithful

Dear old faithful,

What would I do without you?
Where would I be without you?
Time is of the essence, it'll never parish.
Each moment shared I'll truly cherish.
An unbreakable bond beyond belief,
Even the smallest flaws can't be breached.
Truth be told you keep me whole.
Words of encouragement that feed the soul,
Unconditional, nutritional, honest, genuine, everlasting,
heartfelt love...
Only you fit every description above.
Dear old faithful,
Can you hear my cries?
Do you feel my pain?
Face stained from tears oh so dry,
Please hug me tight. Please grab me close.
Ensure what's real is what keeps us close.
Forbidden, foreign, somewhat unusual to most
Who carried, who provided for those extremely long
months,?
Who took honor, pride and joy all at once?
Mom, momma, ma, mother, whichever you choose,
If you didn't get the hints or see the clues...

I love you!

Is there a difference between "Love & Luv"

There is only one fact in comparison between the two words, " Love & Luv". Webster's dictionary has defined Love as an intense affection for another person based on personal or familial ties; A strong affection for or attachment to another person based on regard or shared experiences or interest. The other "luv" is solely opinionated to the individual's standards or beliefs.

If I was to profess any "love" for my mother or any other family member near and dear to my heart, I would "love" them as defined by Webster, an intense affection for another person based on personal or familial ties. That's a strong, pure, genuine, unconditional affectionate "Love". I would also "Love" a companion as defined by webster, a strong affection for or attachment to another person based on regard or shared experiences or interest. This "love" begins as an interest or desirable physical lust, which becomes experienced or shared mental feelings. In turn over a period of time becomes attached "love" for one another emotionally.

When using "Luv" towards a friend or anyone you may not "love" wholeheartedly next week it's best to use the three letter word, which doesn't hold much depth or value. It's just another repetitive expression such as "Bro & Bruh" holding no value or depth. There is no factual evidence or definition behind this "luv" ; it's basic "Ghetto Luv" or slang. You manipulatively "Luv" someone for a while to get what you want for a particular moment in time, then conveniently lose interest in them after your accomplishments are achieved.

   So all in all there is a difference between "Love & Luv". The difference is that "Love" has a meaning that's defined and holds value & depth. "Love" is healed with more purity, genuinely, & unconditionally. While the other "Luv" is more prone to be used as "Ghetto Luv" & slang amongst everyone. "Luv" may not be taken seriously in a text to your lover or spouse.

   "Luv" is cool when used momentarily. It's not cool when there are sentimental qualities expressed for another individual. A wise man once told me that "Love" is the highest form of respect or endearment, it's not used lightly in a greeting or departure. Everybody doesn't deserve those words, I Love You…

"I Did It for the Love"

We live & we learn
We give & we earn
Sometimes we slip, sometimes we fall
Just get back up & give it your all
Who's to say the price we pay
If looks deceives it's ways,
For success we crave & wish
Hunger pains from financial gains
We sacrifice our entire life
To retire broke without a fight
They planted the root that ruled the vice
Never exposing it's costly price
We save for days rainy & hazed
Constantly purchasing ways that keeps us faced
Physically free our mind in a maze
Simply amazed
As we engage
In the most evil ways
All for the love of money...

I Do

If I pledge my life to you,
Would you pledge your life to me?
Would you touch me, tease me?
I don't like to beg, baby please me.
Mentally, physically, emotionally, fulfill my desires.
You spark my soul baby, you truly light my fire.
I'm a thousand, million, billion, trillion, gazillion times yours.
Smell the love seeping through my pores.
Silent nights away from each other
Will only strengthen our bond you'll soon discover
That yes, our commitment is different.
Overflowing with love, excitement dripping,
You clearly don't know what you do to me.
I'm starting to catch the drift when you say, "I got to pee."
Laughing out loud I'm weak as a bitch.
Scratching all over your body,
Let me be the oh shit baby to your itch.
Kiss me through the phone.
Goose bump induced chills from moans
Penetrating oh so slow,
Can you feel me in your stomach?
Stroke, stroke, stroke, stroke, stroke... I'm coming!
All in your world as your faithful husband.
Fuck what the haters say & all the jealousy buzzing.
Family over all, my most prized possession.
You are my queen, soon to be my wife I'm confessing.
Believe in we & stop the unnecessary stressing.

"Growth & Maturity"

Reuniting with old friends after so many years is strange. Finding out the obstacles & chores of someone else is unbelieved. Only the strong survive the trials & tribulations of adversity.

Salute to all the women who stood firm with their men in the time of need....

Salute to all the official men who came home & stood with their women after the storm...

Friends must keep shit real at all times. This leads to lovers keeping shit real and that ultimately leads to husbands & wives inside a circle of trust that's stronger than the weight of the world. A couple represents each other. Woman compliments man & man compliments woman. Longevity is the goal in any serious committed partnership. One hand washes the other and they both wash the face as one. Unity. Working as a unit. We as One. Always allow as much time as needed before jumping into anything, because rushing into something or someone can not be truly genuine. Please make sure the love is sincere, honest, true, pure & unconditional and that the feeling of nothing else outweighs your love for that individual.

It takes a strong man to survive & endure the harsh conditions of prison mentally, physically, and emotionally. It takes an even stronger woman to unconditionally love an individual who's incarcerated to fully understand what comes with prison. Not being able to receive physical support is the hardest when there's so many risky temptations to indulge in. Strength must be exhibited from deep within. Mentally preparing yourself for the return of your best friend, lover or spouse is also stressful. Nevertheless waiting is hard not knowing what to expect & the fear of the unknown begins to set in playing pranks on your mind, body, heart, soul, and relationship.

Should I Ever

    Become a voice like Malcolm or have the heart of Martin...We just want the dream of equality.
Now it's nightmares of black men being gunned down in cycles,as when they were hung by the devious and spiteful. Individuals we describe as white folks, with egotistical animosity fueled rifles,
Political warriors like Black Panthers never lasted, they were extinguished and bottled up by the masses. Indeed our ancestors deserve the medal of recognition for the countless efforts and life taking positions.

Should I Ever

    Start a task without finishing it, remind me of the pig intestines, piss & shit
Our mothers, mother vomit stained outfits, & those who had no choice to quit, pick cotton in blazing heat or get whipped, repeatedly being raped, dignity stripped, impregnated with mixed race babies. Bootlicking house niggas gone crazy.
Brain washing our ladies four hundred years of slavery.

Should I Ever

    Take a knee just know it's a stand for my legacy and what's still yet to come of senseless tragedies. As mass incarceration becomes modern day birth control, with a jackass president being the biggest internet troll, plus mind blowing allegations of sex crimes exposed. lightning

strikes, darkness explodes, An epidemic of opioids is crushing the nation ass too much waiting patiently becomes procrastination,...
OMG! WTF! SMH.
Positive energy we must generate

Should I Ever

Educate our youth on the shameful hate. I'll teach them to respect, protect & procreate. Informing that knowledge is key, Giving understanding to the power of words, that we are so often afraid of free speech to speak. Allowing meaningful conversations to decrease our reach. Acknowledging our daughters as Queens & never a Bitches. Holding our sons to the highest apex, pushing beyond the furthest extent.
Enriching the minds of our fruit begins with the soil. Quality over quantity empowering future King's & Queens becoming Royal.

Shell Shocked

Shots ring out...
 Kids cry out...
Scrambling, spreading like roaches to find a clear route.
"Everybody Down", somebody shouts.
"Ooh, Ahh! Shit! Fuck! Damn! Ouch!"
"Where's my baby? Find my baby, please!"
Scuffed shoes, scraped bruises & bloody knees.
Dirty white tees. Grass stained jeans.
Traumatizing, deadly, life treating screams...
Red & blue lights appear on the scene.
Brightly glaring, shiny high beams.
Witnesses approach, reenacting the drama,
From a muffler backfiring on an old ass honda.

"State of Incarceration"

As I search for answers my mind is puzzled,
Walking through this maze of dust looking for a piece of life to guzzle,
Thirsty for knowledge, wisdom, & ultimate understanding
At times daily obstacles can be very much demanding,
Steady & focus as my path seems clear,
Where am I, why am I, what am I truly doing here?
Trapped on the darkside, but I can see the light.
Mentally incriminating mindset fighting to do right,
Confined amongst the extremely worst that weren't placed inside a hearse.
Animalistic caveman reactions tend to disburse,
Insane movements amongst a society within.
The only way to escape is to release my pain though this pen.
Allowing the ink to cry out loud as it substitutes my tears.
The unknown upon reunitement is one of my biggest fears.

Magnetic Connection

My soul yearns for your energy
Tingling shockwaves strike when we're in close proximity
The brightest star in my solar system
I'm your knowledge
Your my wisdom
Combined we'll produce a powerful understanding
Cocky, arrogant, confident, respect demanding
You possess the powers and abilities
Of peace, relaxation, & tranquility
The queen of my universe
U-N-I-verse the worlds worst
The greatest reflection of GOD, was you woman
Humanly designed specifically for me

Happily Dedicated

To my bride to be,

        Open your eyes and see
        That we
        Are specially made to be
        No matter how challenging it may seem
        Remember that we're one great team
        Only in your wildest dreams could you imagine
        That love would come in the form of me
        Pure passion
        Dedicated specifically for my queen
        Unconditionally genuine by all means
        Thank you for being so amazing
        Every day with you is a special occasion
        Kiss me baby, hug me too
        I miss u and will forever love u

Safe

Realizing that you are deeply hurt makes me frustrated
Even more so, as my actions can't really be shown due to my situation
Stay strong no matter what, hold your head up with pride and joy
Congratulate yourself from time to time on your smallest achievements
Uplifting yourself also motivates you to reach personal goals
Encourage yourself daily to do your best
Determination should always be implemented in your mind

Forget all your past heartaches and pain
Reunite yourself with the world
Only one person will love you unconditionally and that's me
Male changes are needed, no more sabotage for me

However, life is not over just yet
Eventually, all wounds heal at some point in time
Lessons learned, we've all had our share
Learn, love, and live life to the fullest

Uncovering Verse Discovery

When I thought it couldn't get any worse,
It did……

I cried thinking I could never find someone that truly loves me,
I did…..

Never million years did I think I wouldn't be able to cry at a challenging point in my life,
I didn't….

I found relief being cherished by you,
I am...

Did I ever believe I was appreciated,
I didn't…..

I wasn't dead but I was loved genuinely by individuals that people say they couldn't or how,
I was...

Throughout it all, I found you
Who made a difference in my life, gave me strength & motivation when I couldn't…..

No one may ever understand, but I do
I love u…….

Some people say how and why,
I say why not….

My Brother is your Brother

Reflection of lost souls gone to soon;
I am Trayvon Martin:

Please don't worry yourself when I leave your presence
Just hope and pray the lord showers me with his blessings
Anything is bound to happen, like a conflict with a stranger
Confrontation could place my life in serious danger
I didn't create this problem, I was being oppressed
Now my parents have to live with one less child
Only because I was targeted as a
"punk ass thug"
Who is always high and most likely on drugs
Being stereotyped as the youth is now days basic
But trust me it was much more than that, my attacker was racist
Not seen as a hate crime or even murder
Not guilty was the verdict truly unheard of
As the world realizes the Justice system never gave a damn
We need to come together and hold shit down
Now that's classified as standing your ground

" The law of Attraction"

The law of attraction between men and women is (physicalism- the view that all that exists is ultimately physical) character, demeanors, and or personality. The energy you give off attracts like minded individuals with the same forcefield, good or bad. You determine the persons whom you connect/attract (vibrantly-displaying, marked by, or caused by vibration; throbbing or pulsing with energy or activity). Quizzically, most women pass a skill of intimidation simply by not smiling. Some men take that as she doesn't want to be bothered, she's being evil, she thinks she's too good to speak, or even she thinks she's better than them.

These syndromes are typical within weak men having insecurities. Feel they're not secure or safe, unsound; unstable; lacking self confidence or uncertainty in situations. They often simply need a kind word from another. First and foremost you must be confident within yourself before approaching any situation let alone a strong independent, confident woman. If your energy isn't positive or strong in nature when coming across a confident woman, she can feel his uncertainty and lack of confidence. Men that are cocky, arrogant, and overconfident are looked at as egotistical jerks.

Women who focus on the uncertainties of where they are and what they possess in life tend to allow men to trample over top of them because they don't know their own powers. Worthy of much more than sexual favors, disrespect, betrayal, manipulation, and or chaotic circumstances. A treasure isn't a treasure until someone discovers it's worth, holding it with high regards amongst all. The unbeknownst woman accepts anything she receives due to histories of being misled and miseducated, having misconceptions or notions learned within society traditions.

Love Doctor X

My ex say it ain't like dat but I know it's dat,
She's known for bucking, so I can't bet dat,
If u like it....
I love it..
I guess...
Self preservation sweetheart,
Focus on what's absolutely best for yourself
For real, For real
No one will ever love you like you
There's a treasure map to your life
You need only to follow the clues
They say love is pain and pain is love
Stupidity is the most shameful love
Never appear to be desperate or eager
It's a mental sickness,
No symptoms No fever
Official diagnosis...Love is blind
Recommendation: plenty of alone time,
Follow up when the crying stops
Only questions or untouched spots
Just follow your heart...

Have a wonderful day....
Love always...
A good friend...
Love, Doctor X...

Say Her Name, Say Her Name

Look into eyes of a man that's full of pain
Even when the sun shines, I wonder will it rain
They say I'm just stuck in my ways, so who's to blame?
All my life I was destined for greatness,
but it never came
So is it my fault that my mentality towards life hasn't changed
Praise the Lord, worship the devil, it's all the same
It's just the baddest bitch with the super phat ass, cute face who left no name
Headed down a one way road in a rush
Hopping to find a silver spoon instead I found a copper spoon that was majority rust
Shit! Don't feel sorry for me, I didn't listen
Just know karma is a bitch, if I forgot to mention

"Uncertainties"

Dear you,

If you are reading this, you're special
Maybe not.
Who's to say that I even like you?
Maybe I like you a little
Or maybe I'm just bored tricking myself into believing I like you
Maybe I would like to get to know you
Maybe you should know that I want you
Maybe you could take a few seconds to get to know me
Maybe I'm not so bad
Or maybe I'll find out you aren't what I expected.

Dear you,

Maybe the way you speak intrigues me
Maybe your radiance attracts me
Maybe it's the way you gloss your lips
Or the seductive sway of your hips
Maybe your outspoken personality turns me on
Maybe I just need to express this
Maybe I'm letting my imagination run wild
Maybe I'm dreaming beyond grey clouds
Maybe I shouldn't shoot my shot
Or maybe I'm way out of bounds

Dear you,

Maybe you can't view the signs
Or maybe you're totally blind
Maybe not
Maybe I'm not your type
Maybe I'm not worthy to enter your life
Maybe your circle of trust is already too tight
Maybe you aren't worth my time
Maybe these were the most wasted moments of my life
Maybe I should stop pursuing
Maybe that's what I'll do with guarantees of never looking back

Dear you,

If you're reading this now it's too late
Fuck you

Can't help but wait...

The thought of us making love drives me insane at times.
The smell of you takes me beyond imagination,
simply blows my mind.
Can't help but wait until your lips are pressed against mine.
Face down, ass up, kissing every inch of your behind.
Nasty, some might say.
My reply, " I just can't help it"
Can't wait until your juices are splashed onto my dick
Lay back and let me take you on this spectacular ride.
Buckle up and enjoy, scream out or cry out with pride.
Can't help but wait until you say it's mine.
Every part of you from the bottom of your feet to the very
top of your spine,
Eat this, lick that, shed joyful tears of pain
Can't help but wait for you to stop playing games
Until then, my mind, body, and soul will be filled with pain.
Can't help but wait. Can't help but wait. Can't help but wait.

The Inability And Incapability To Love Never Allow Your Past To Define You...

Well as I stated, I would love us to focus on bettering ourselves. Dropping bad habits, picking up new good ones for the sake of progression and never looking back at what once was. Your potential is worth more than you know at this moment. A woman's worth is measured up to her expectations that she has within life, her worth as well as her wants should coexist. If she's worth the world she shouldn't want anything less than the world for herself. If she's only experienced disrespect, betrayal, and drama, she's more prone to frustration, chaos, and confusion brainwashing herself into becoming numb to hurt ultimately falling in love with pain.

Her misunderstanding of "love" leaves her misunderstood in the eyes of others. What she thinks is normal is actually insanity. Her normalcy is suffering from abuse and pain, both physical or verbal, which is a serious mental illness.

* Insanity: serious mental disorder or derangement impairing one's ability to function safely and normally.

Never allow anyone to degrade or belittle you. Accepting these things will lessen your worth, break your spirit and confidence. It will have you feeling insecure and powerless. Self empowerment is to empower one's self no matter the situation or circumstances.

As a scorned woman all men may appear to be similar, whether it's the way he speaks, dresses, laughs or presents himself. Good men don't stand a chance without proving himself beyond her normality, truly unusual unexpected politeness, kind gestures, compliments, opening doors, pulling out chairs, etc.

Most men look for similarities in between his woman and mother because his mother was the first love in his life. He's going to treat both with the utmost love, honor, and respect as possible. Trust me shivery isn't dead.

*Scorn: a contempt or disdain felt towards a person or object considered despicable or inferior.The expression of such an attitude in behavior or speech; derision, one treated or spoken of with contempt.

Breaking down the barriers of a woman after she's suffered painful experiences throughout her years is like pulling teeth with tweezers, the possibilities are slim to none. The trust factor has been shattered into tiny shards in the form of: heartache, betrayal, disloyalty, lies, and tears. The wall must be broken down systematically, piece by piece until the comfortable level is reached. Please remember not to push too hard or she may crawl back into her shell shutting down with no explanation, pulling away is easy for this specific woman. Attachment is hard, unusual and painful.

In my opinion the woman is the dominant species of human beings. Women are beautiful creatures who come in all shapes, sizes, colors, and forms. It's said that men can't live with them and can't live without them. The woman must carry a fetus for nine months, push that fetus out of her overly stretched womb for hours. Painful as it may seem and sound, men couldn't possibly imagine or pretend to understand the strength and pain tolerance of our women. The woman bleeds for several days cleaning herself out monthly like clockwork. In most instances a woman is the better half of a man, she gives him a different type of motivational drive.

    Some women use what they got to get what they want. Please don't continue to keep selling yourself short sisters. You're so much more than a lay. Women know your worth, value, potential, strengths, abilities, and wants, then figure out a solution to get it all.

"The Everlasting Impression of on Incarcerated Mind of Man"

Always use your mind as your strength. The everlasting impression of the mind can and will show you complete wisdom and knowledge of one's self or the incapabilities of an immature mind.

Mind over matter is the case when dealing with anything in life. It's truly easier said than done. Always approach any situation with a clear and open mind, unless it's a totally misleading presumption of one's dignity or character. Which means, "Blatant disrespect will not be tolerated, Period." Never allow the assassination of ones self.

Remember to always remain humble through the trials and tribulations life may place upon you. Accomplishments are to be celebrated after victory is prevailed. Humbleness is the key to achieving greatness and still this is also mind over matter. Knowing and understanding that if you generate positive thoughts and energy and put your mind to it, in a matter of time you will prosper. Negative thoughts usually lead to failure. Self control is having control over oneself physically, spiritually, emotionally as well as mentally. Mind over matter.

The mind is the strongest part of the body. It has the ability to feel, think and reason with every other part of the body. It takes charge of the human structure carefully paying attention. Matter is described as something that deals with problems. Now going back to grade school matter is the substance things are made of, something that takes up space and has weight. Knowing and understanding that the mind controls the problems, I understand the saying, "mind over matter."

    The matter and fact of anything takes up space and can weigh heavy on the brain, mind over matter. The substance of learning the facts and problems allows the mind to feel, think, as well as reason with life as it understands it. The mind is of two forms, a strong mind and a weak mind. A weak mind gives into anything it may come across, as a strong mind may think and reason with the situation until it's best understood.

    The first impression of oneself means a lot, it speaks volumes. So always think, speak and act accordingly to how you want the world to perceive and respond to your character.

Always I remain:
Respectful, loyal ,wise,
Humble and true to
Myself ...
Chip

Acknowledgements/ Thank You's

    I want to first start off by sending my unconditional love to my mother who has never turned her back or given up on me. Thank You Momma I Love You untraditionally. To the Queen in my life who made it possible for me to share my words & thoughts to the world. Thanks babe, we are in it so let's get it. To the elder wise men I have been blessed to meet throughout my journey while doing time, I truly appreciate y'all for guiding me in the right direction and for sharing everlasting knowledge & wisdom with me until I gained understanding of self.

    Thank You to all who have traveled with me throughout this journey, & to all of you who have left allowing me to view life in a different perspective. I truly appreciate all of you. FAMILY isn't always blood relatives & mine has been one helluva support system. Love is love, but loyalty is a must!

Being incarnated since age 19, now 33, I have struggled. As you read my opinionated thoughts, inner conversations, and experiences throughout my incarnation you will see the evolution of a young man who's been lost, broken, hurt and ultimately forced to become a man behind bars. This is no one's fault but my own. I chose the wrong path leading me into this cold world of reality. Constantly reading and educating myself with guidance of a few good brothers helped me to become the man I am today. Thank you to everyone who chose to pick my thoughts up deciding to enter my cold hearted world, yet still a man with a tender soul.

Milton Keynes UK
Ingram Content Group UK Ltd.
UKHW020629171124
2899UKWH00042B/396